Detective Dog
and the Ghost

Detective Dog
and the Ghost

Written by Leslie McGuire
Illustrated by Mitchell Rose

© 2020 SANDVIKS HOP, Inc. All Rights Reserved.
Published by Hooked on Phonics, a division of Sandviks HOP, Inc.
Originally published in a different form in 1998.

No part of this publication may be reproduced, stored in any retrieval system, or
transmitted, in any form or by any means, electronic, mechanical or otherwise, without prior written
permission of the publisher.

Hooked on Phonics and associated logos are trademarks and/or registered trademarks of
Sandviks HOP, Inc., Danbury, CT.

Printed in China.

SP20001816NOV2020

Contents

1. There Are No Ghosts   9

2. I Do Not Like This   21

3. It's a Ghost!   29

4. I Get It!   39

Special Words

Special words help make this story fun. Practice reading them here and look for them in the story.

cobwebs

detective

ghost

hanging

house

kitten

odd

skids

trap

white

1 There Are No Ghosts

I am Detective Dog. I look for lost pets. I get the pets back.

BAM! BAM! BAM!
I go to the door.
"Who is it?" I say.
"It's Jack Cat and Max Fox," says Jack. Jack looks upset.
I say, "What's up, Jack?"

"My pet kitten is lost," says Jack. "Can you get him back?"

"Yes, I can," I say. "Where did you last see him?"

"In my yard," says Jack. "I was hanging sheets on the line to dry. But my kitten is not there now."

"I heard sounds coming from the house on top of the hill," says Max.

"There is a ghost in that house," says Jack. "I bet the ghost got my kitten."

"There are no ghosts," I say,
"but I will get the kitten back."

I set out for the house on the hill. I need to get Jack's kitten back and check out this ghost. Jack and Max do not know it, but there are NO ghosts!

I huff and puff up the hill. I do not see a ghost. But I do see a big house. It looks like a mess!

I go up to the house. Hmmm. There is no lock. I go into the house. That is when there is a C-R-A-C-K!
What is that?

I look here and there. Then I see an odd white thing by a box!
"Now what?" I think. "What can this white thing be?"

 # I Do Not Like This

I go to check.
Then ZIP!
The white thing is GONE!

Did it go that way?
I look in back of
the box.
No white thing.
That's when...

WAP! ZAP! WAP!
I look! I see it! The white thing skids by me and zips into the kitchen!

I do not want to, but I go into the kitchen.

There are lots of cobwebs in there! Yuck! Cobwebs stick to me. I do not like this.

I see a jug with a big crack in it. Then...

WAP! BAP! THUD!

The white thing zips by my leg! I trip over the jug and slip. The jug spills. Yuck!

I do not get it! I know there are no ghosts.

"THERE ARE NO GHOSTS!" I say.

That's when I see the white thing whiz by me! It goes up! WAY up! It goes up to the top of a shelf.

I go out.

3 It's a Ghost!

I need to sit down! I need to think. I get out my pad.

"If the white thing can go up…," I say, "is it a ghost?"

A ghost?

I think I need to go up and see if it's a ghost or not.

"Here I come," I say.

I do NOT want to do this. But I am Detective Dog. I do what I say. I will get to the bottom of this.

That's when...

BONG! BONG! BONG!
Ack! I run. I run smack into a big clock! I look up. The ghost is on top of the clock!

I panic and drop my hat.
Then I run into the door. I fall
down. That's when I
see it!

"I bet there's a way to get rid of ghosts," I say. "I will go back to my house and look it up!"
That's when…

CLICK! CLICK! CLICK!
The clicks come from the stairs.
I look up. It's the ghost!

I bet it wants me to come up the stairs!

What if it's a trap?

4 I Get It!

"You can run, and you can fly," I say to the ghost, "but you cannot trap ME! I am Detective Dog! I will come up there NOW!"

Up I go.
I check the steps.

I make quick stops.

I look this way and that way.

At the top... I stop!
I see something white on the floor.
It is moving. Is it the ghost?
What will happen to me now?

But what is this thing? It's just a white sheet! What is in it?

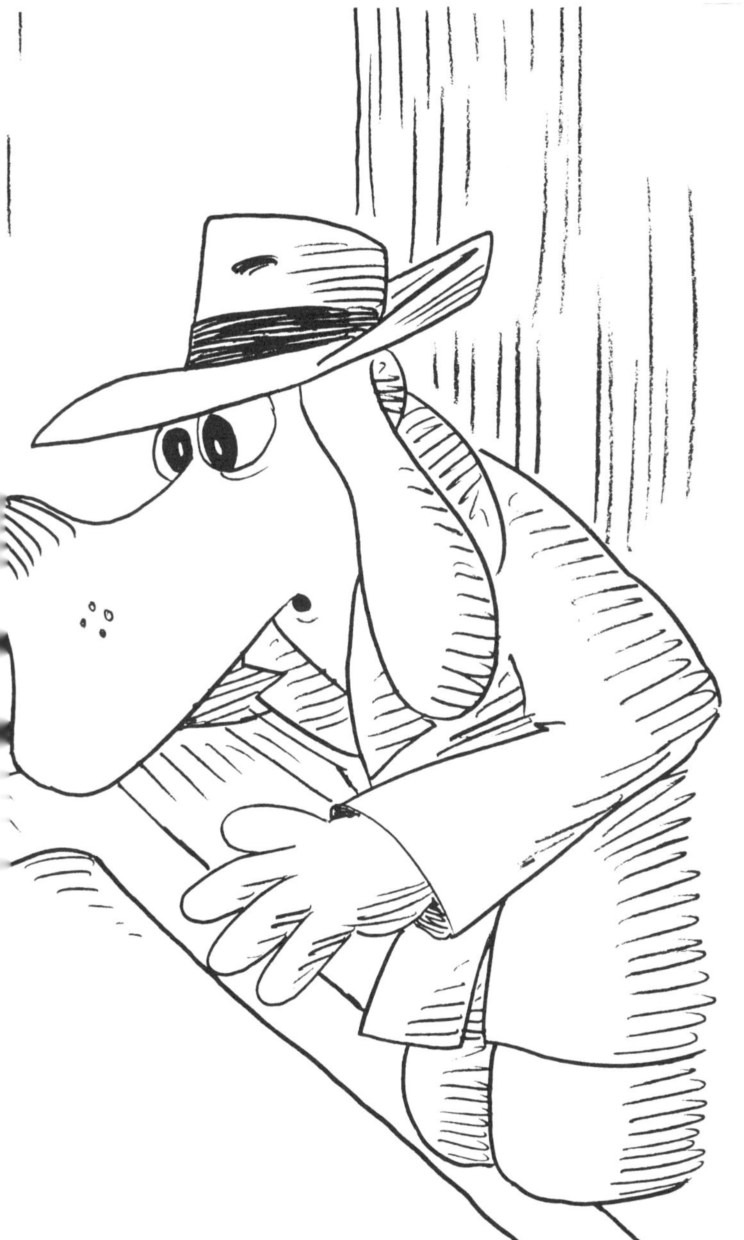

It's a kitten!
NOW I get it!

The kitten was
trapped in the sheet!
There are no ghosts.

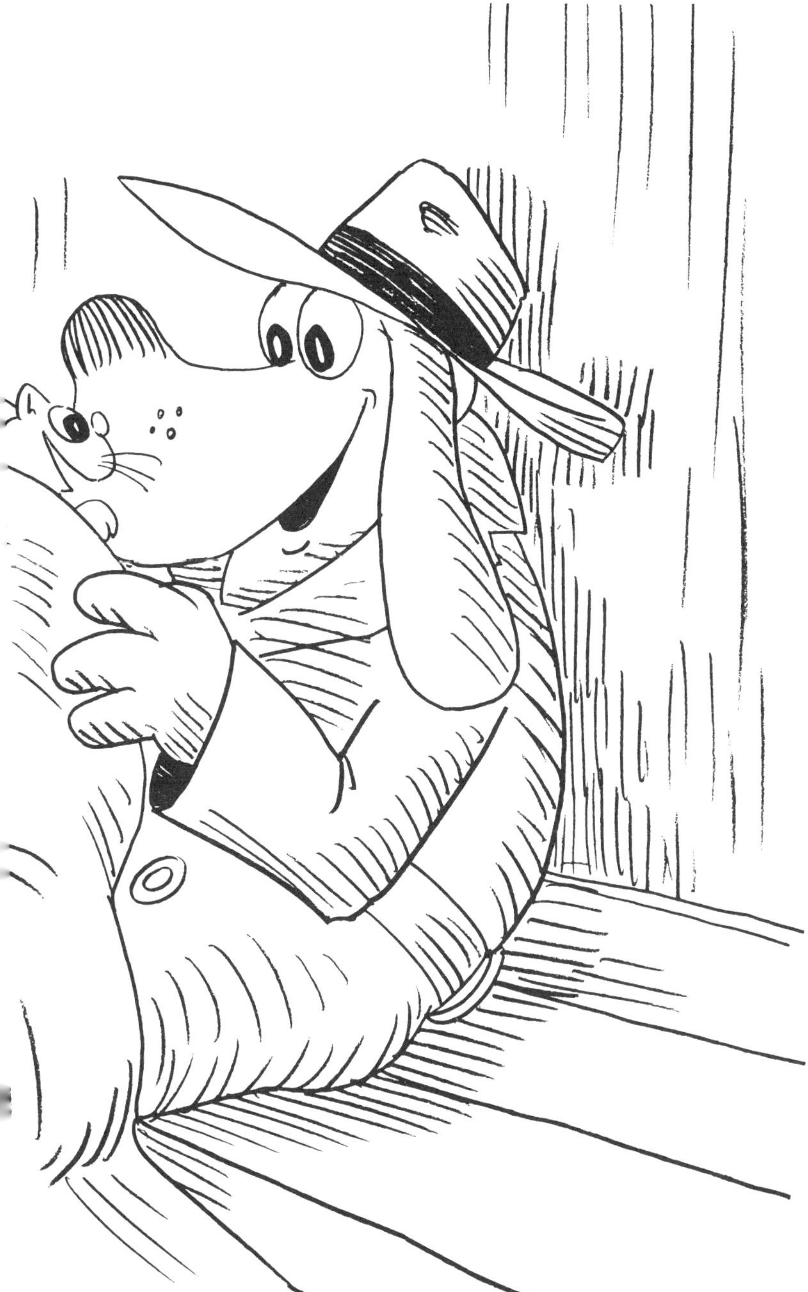

That's when the kitten says,
Meow, MEOW! MEOW!

"I bet you are Jack's kitten,"
I say. "He will be glad to have you back! Let's go!"

"Thanks, Detective Dog," says Jack. "You got my kitten back!"

"That's a good thing," says Max. "You are a good detective!"

"Yes," I say, "and…
THERE ARE NO GHOSTS!"